THE LITTLE RED BOOK OF

GRANDMOTHER'S WISDOM

THE LITTLE RED BOOK OF

GRANDMOTHER'S WISDOM

Edited by Holly Rubino

Skyhorse Publishing

Skyhorse Publishing books may be purchased in bulk at special discounts for sales promotion, corporate gifts, fund-raising, or educational purposes. Special editions can also be created to specifications. For details, contact the Special Sales Department, Skyhorse Publishing, 307 West 36th Street, 11th Floor, New York, NY 10018 or info@skyhorsepublishing.com.

Skyhorse® and Skyhorse Publishing® are registered trademarks of Skyhorse Publishing, Inc.®, a Delaware corporation.

Visit our website at www.skyhorsepublishing.com.

10 9 8 7 6 5 4 3 2 1

Library of Congress Cataloging-in-Publication Data is available on file.

ISBN: 978-1-62636-088-4

Printed in China

For Frances—

I wish I had told you how remarkable you were more often.

"Truth be told, being a grandma is as close as we ever get to perfection. The ultimate warm sticky bun with plump raisins and nuts. Clouds nine, ten, and eleven."

—Bryna Nelson Paston

Contents

Introduction

My Grandma Huber was a spitfire, who even into her eighties could haul the air conditioner from the basement to the third floor and install it herself. She spoke fluent Polish and made the best pierogies I've ever eaten. Whenever I asked her for the recipe, she always said, "You just use a little of this, and a little of that . . ." (Grandmothers seem to be notorious for not writing down ingredients.)

Most people in this day and age see their grandmothers only a few times a year, usually during the holidays. I had the good fortune of living with mine in her home at 5 Bergen Street in Garfield, New Jersey, for a few years. The "Huber Hotel" is what she liked to call it after having countless relatives (including one very stern mother-in-law) take up residence there. At that point in my life, I was working during the day and going to graduate school at night. I don't know what I would have done without the laundry and cooking services that Frances provided, let alone her unwavering encouragement. Even though she didn't finish high school, I never felt that she begrudged me my education.

Back then I might have thought how pathetic it was to spend Saturday evenings on the couch with her watching *The*

Golden Girls. Or trying to digest kielbasa at ten o'clock at night. Or having to repeat almost everything I said (she was a little hard of hearing). But those are all things I remember fondly now. There's something about enduring hardships together that can really bring people close.

After I moved away, there was a big adjustment for both of us. She used to tell me that every time she heard the train's whistle on Plauderville Avenue in the evening, she would expect me to bound through the door soon after, hungry for dinner (even the kielbasa). I missed being taken care of by such a warm and sweet person. I guess there's always a little heartbreak that comes with love.

My grandmother was a very special person to me, and, even though they might not tell you this very often, I suspect you are likewise very special to your grandchildren. If this book makes you feel some of that specialness, then the many voices captured here have done good service.

Introduction

Chapter 1

Congratulations, You're a Grandma!

Whether this is your first or twenty-first time, becoming a grandmother is a wonderful life-changing experience that can very quickly elevate you to the status of wise, all-knowing one. Here are some words to remind you just how noble and inspiring a figure you are.

• • •

"When a child is born, so are grandmothers."
—JUDITH LEVY

• • •

"So many things we love are you!"
—ANNE MORROW LINDBERGH

• • •

"Becoming a grandmother is wonderful. One moment you're just a mother. The next you are all-wise and prehistoric."
—PAM BROWN

• • •

"If you would civilize a man, begin with his grandmother."
—VICTOR HUGO

• • •

Grandmothers are . . .

"moms with lots of frosting."

"just antique little girls."

"old on the outside, but young on the inside."

"a little bit parent, a little bit teacher, and a little bit best friend."

"the footsteps to the future generations."

"are a delightful blend of laughter, caring deeds, wonderful stories, and love."

"wonderful mothers—with lots of practice."

"people who make the world a little softer, a little kinder, a little warmer."

"mothers who have a second chance."

"those who hold our tiny hands for just a while, but our hearts forever."

"family members who never run out of hugs or cookies."

• • •

Congratulations, You're a Grandma!

Digital Vision/Thinkstock

"It is as grandmothers that our mothers come into the
fullness of their grace."
—CHRISTOPHER MORLEY

• • •

"The Queen Mother, with a lifetime's popularity, seemed
incapable of a bad performance as national grandmother—
warm, smiling, human, understanding, she embodied everything the public could want of its grandmother."
—JOHN PEARSON

• • •

"We have become a grandmother."
—MARGARET THATCHER

• • •

iStockphoto/Thinkstock

"She seems to have had the ability to stand firmly on the rock of her past while living completely and unregretfully in the present."
—MADELEINE L'ENGLE

• • •

"Grandparents are a family's greatest treasure, the founders of a loving legacy, the greatest storytellers, the keepers of traditions that linger on in cherished memory. Grandparents are the family's strong foundation. Their very special love sets them apart. Through happiness and sorrow, through their special love and caring, grandparents keep a family close at heart."
—AUTHOR UNKNOWN

• • •

"You are the sun, grandma, you are the sun in my life."
—KITTY TSUI

• • •

Congratulations, You're a Grandma!

"If becoming a grandmother was only a matter of choice, I should advise every one of you straight away to become one. There is no fun for old people like it!"
—HANNAH WHITALL SMITH

• • •

"Most grandmas have a touch of the scallywag."
—HELEN THOMSON

• • •

"If your baby is 'beautiful and perfect, never cries or fusses, sleeps on schedule and burps on demand, an angel all the time,' you're the grandma."
—TERESA BLOOMINGDALE

• • •

"Dear Grandmamma, with what we give / We humbly pray that you may live / For many, many happy years: / Although you bore us all to tears."
—HILAIRE BELLOC

• • •

"Soup simmering, music of idle gossip, yammering kids,
domestic chaos—long adjusted to this rolling scene,
you show them your lofty calm."
—GOTTFRIED KELLER

• • •

"If God had intended us to follow recipes, He wouldn't
have given us grandmothers."
—LINDA HENLEY

• • •

"Let's bring back grandmothers! A real family consists of
three generations. It's time Americans stopped worrying about
interference and being a burden on the children
and regrouped under one roof."
—FLORENCE KING

• • •

"If grandmas hadn't existed, kids would have inevitably
invented them."
—ARTHUR KORNHABER, M.D.

• • •

Congratulations, You're a Grandma!

Steve Mason/Photodisc/Thinkstock

"Being a grandmother is our last chance to act like a kid without being accused of being in our second childhood."
—JANET LANESE

• • •

"It's funny what happens when you become a grandparent. You start to act all goofy and do things you never thought you'd do. It's terrific."
—MIKE KRZYZEWSKI

• • •

"A grandmother is a babysitter who watches the kids instead of the television."
—AUTHOR UNKNOWN

• • •

"Never have children, only grandchildren."
—GORE VIDAL

• • •

George Doyle/Stockbyte/Thinkstock

"A mother becomes a true grandmother the day she stops noticing the terrible things her children do because she is so enchanted with the wonderful things her grandchildren do."
—LOIS WYSE

• • •

"A grandmother pretends she doesn't know who you are on Halloween."
—ERMA BOMBECK

• • •

"Even the devil's grandmother was a nice girl when she was young."
—GERMAN PROVERB

• • •

"A house needs a grandma in it."
—LOUISA MAY ALCOTT

• • •

"When the grandmothers of today hear the word
'Chippendales,' they don't necessarily think of chairs."
—JEAN KERR

• • •

"Didn't we, like our grandchildren, begin with a childhood we
thought would never end? Now, all of a sudden, I'm older than
my parents were when I thought they were old."
—LOIS WYSE

• • •

"It's amazing how grandparents seem so young
once you become one."
—AUTHOR UNKNOWN

• • •

"My grandmother is over eighty and still doesn't need
glasses. Drinks right out of the bottle."
—HENNY YOUNGMAN

• • •

Congratulations, You're a Grandma!

"Truth be told, there's nothing better than being a grandparent. All our elders know this and it is evidenced by that twinkle in their eyes. Of course, they know more than they let on—life's secrets have come to them through time, experience, and patience."
—AUTHOR UNKNOWN

• • •

"Our mothers and grandmothers . . . moving to music not yet written."
—ALICE WALKER

• • •

"Soon I will be an old, white-haired lady, into whose lap someone places a baby, saying, 'Smile, Grandma!'—I, who myself so recently was photographed on my grandmother's lap."
—LIV ULLMANN

• • •

"You do not really understand something unless you can explain it to your grandmother."
—AUTHOR UNKNOWN

• • •

"Some of the world's best educators are grandparents."
—CHARLES W. SHEDD

• • •

"Grandmothers are voices of the past and role models of the present. Grandmothers open the doors to the future."
—HELEN KETCHUM

• • •

"Whether she is a homemaker or career woman, all a grandmother wants is her family's love and respect as a productive individual who has much to contribute."
—JANET LANESE

• • •

iStockphoto/Thinkstock

"My grandmother started walking five miles a day when she was sixty. She's ninety-seven now, and we don't know where the hell she is."
—ELLEN DEGENERES

• • •

"Her grandmother, as she gets older, is not fading, but rather becoming more concentrated."
—PAULETTE BATES ALDEN

• • •

"A married daughter with children puts you in danger of being catalogued as a first edition."
—AUTHOR UNKNOWN

• • •

"A friend of mine was asked how she liked having her first great-grandchild. 'It was wonderful,' she replied, 'until I suddenly realized that I was the mother of a grandfather!'"
—ROBERT L. RICE, M.D.

• • •

"Look, how they scold me for all my loving and tippling, now that the silvery edges shine forth from my brow!"
—ABY YAHYA

• • •

"A grandmother is a safe haven."
—SUZETTE HADEN ELGIN

• • •

"No one . . . who has not known that inestimable privilege
can possibly realize what good fortune it is to grow up
in a home where there are grandparents."
—SUZANNE LA FOLLETTE

• • •

"Sometimes our grandmas and grandpas are
like grand-angels."
—LEXIE SAIGE

• • •

"We should all have one person who knows how to bless us
despite the evidence. Grandmother was that person to me."
—PHYLLIS THEROUX

• • •

Congratulations, You're a Grandma!

"Grandparents bring about a side that you probably wish that's how your parents dealt with you while you were a child. Abundance of indulgence and unwavering love."
—AUTHOR UNKNOWN

• • •

"A grandma's name is little less in love than is the doting title of a mother."
—WILLIAM SHAKESPEARE

• • •

"Even now / I am not old. / I never think of it, and yet / I am a grandmother to eleven grandchildren."
—GRANDMA MOSES

• • •

"Holding these babies in my arms makes me realize the miracle my husband and I began."
—BETTY FORD

• • •

"A garden of love grows in a grandmother's heart."
—AUTHOR UNKNOWN

• • •

"When it seems the world can't understand, your
grandmother's there to hold your hand."
—JOYCE K. ALLEN LOGAN

• • •

"Grandma always made you feel she had been waiting to see
just you all day and now the day was complete."
—MARCY DEMAREE

• • •

"Now that I've reached the age where I need my children more
than they need me, I really understand how grand
it is to be a grandmother."
—MARGARET WHITLAM

• • •

"Unconditional positive regard is rarely given by anyone
except a grandparent."
—AUTHOR UNKNOWN

• • •

"Uncles and aunts, and cousins, are all very well, and fathers
and mothers are not to be despised; but a grandmother, at
holiday time, is worth them all."
—FANNY FERN

• • •

"Just about the time a woman thinks her work is done,
she becomes a grandmother."
—EDWARD H. DRESCHNACK

• • •

"There's no place like home except Grandma's."
—AUTHOR UNKNOWN

• • •

CHAPTER 2

A Grandmother by Any Other Name Is Still as Sweet

Having trouble deciding what you'd like the grandkids to call you? Here are a couple of lists that contain traditional and contemporary variations on "grandmother," as well as a comprehensive assemblage of names from around the world.

Traditional Grandmother Names:

Big Mom	Grandmom	Mema	Noni
Gram	Grandmother	Memaw	Ona
Gramma	Grannie	Mimsey	
Grammy	Ma or Maw	Mom-Mom	
Grams	Mamey	Nana	
Grandma	Mamo	Nanny	
Grandmama	MawMaw	Ne-ma	

Fun Nicknames for Grandma:

Bamma	Gabby	Jamma	MeMom	NotherMother
BeBe	GaGa	Lola	Mia	Nooni
Bella	GiGi	Lovey	Mim	Snuggums
Birdie	Glammy	Mamabear	Mimi	Tootsie
Bunny	G-Ma	Mamacita	Momo	Unni
Cookie	G-Mom	Mammi	Momsy	
Foxy	Honey	MayMay	Nina	

iStockphoto/Thinkstock

Grandmothers around the Globe:

Aboriginal

>Australian formal: Garrimaay
>
>Australian (paternal): Mamaay
>
>Australian (maternal): Momu
>
>Polynesian Maori dialect: TipunaWahine

African

>Berber dialect: Henna
>
>Botswanan: Nkuku
>
>Shona dialect: Ambuya
>
>Swahili: Bibi, Nyanya
>
>Venda dialect: Makhulu
>
>Xhosa dialect: Umakhulu
>
>Zulu dialect: Ugogo
>
>Afrikaans: Ouma

Albanian: Gjyshe

American Indian

>Cherokee: E-Ni-Si
>
>Cheyenne: Neske'e
>
>Eskimo, Inupiaq dialect: Aanaga
>
>Navajo (maternal): Ma'saani
>
>Navajo (paternal): Nali'
>
>Ojibway: Nookmis, Nookomis

Arabic

    Formal: Jaddah, Jiddah

    Informal: Teta

Armenian: Tatik

Basque: Amona

Belarusen: Babka

Breton: Mamm-gozh

Cajun: MawMaw

Catalan: Àvia, Iaia

Croatian: Baka

Chinese

    Formal: Zu mu

    Informal: Nainai (for paternal grandmother), Lao lao (for maternal grandmother)

    Variations: Waizu mu, Waipo, Po po

Danish

    Formal: Bedstemoder

    Paternal: Farmor

    Maternal: MorMor

iStockphoto/Thinkstock

Dutch: Grootmoeder

Esperanto: Avin

Estonian: Vanaema

Farsi: MadarBozorg

Filipino

> Formal: Apohangbabae
>
> Informal: Lola, Inang
>
> Variations: Indang, Nanang, Ingkong, Nanay

Finnish: Isoaiti, Mummo

Flemish

> Formal: Grootmoeder
>
> Informal: Bomma

French

> Formal: Grand-mère
>
> Informal: Grand-maman
>
> Variations: Gra-mère, Mémé, Mamé

French Canadian

> Formal: Mémé
>
> Informal: Mémère
>
> Variations: Mamie

German

>Formal: Grossmutter
>
>Informal: Oma
>
>Variations: Omi

Greek

>Formal: Yia-Yia
>
>Informal: Ya-Ya
>
>Variations: Nona

Hawaiian

>Formal: Kuku Wahine
>
>Informal: Tutu
>
>Variations: Kapuna

Hebrew

>Formal: Savta
>
>Informal: Bubbe, Bube, Bubbie, Bubby(Yiddish)
>
>Variations: Savah, Sabta

Hungarian

>Formal: Nagyanya
>
>Informal: Yanya, Anya
>
>Icelandic: Amma

iStockphoto/Thinkstock

Indian

> Bengali (paternal): Thakur-ma
>
> Bengali (maternal): Dida, Didima
>
> Hindi: Daadima
>
> Southwestern: Ajji
>
> Urdu (paternal): Daadi
>
> Urdu (maternal): Nanni

Indonesian: Nenek

Irish

> Formal: Seanmháthair
>
> Informal: Maimeó
>
> Variations: Móraí, Mavoureen

Italian

> Formal: Nonna
>
> Informal: Nonnina
>
> Variations: Nonni

Japanese

> Formal: Obaasan
>
> Informal: Baasan, Baa-baa
>
> Variations: Sobo, Soba

Korean: Halmoni

Latvian: Vecmate

Lebanese: Sitti

Lithuanian: Senele, Mociute

Malagasy: Nenibe

Maltese: Nanna

Norwegian: Bestemor, Godmor

> Paternal: Farmor
>
> Maternal: MorMor

Polish

> Formal: Babcia
>
> Informal: Babciu
>
> Variations: Babunia, Babula, Babusia, Baba, Busia

Portuguese

> Formal: Avó
>
> Informal: Vovó
>
> Variations: Avozinha, Vo

Romanian: Bunica

Russian

> Formal: Babushka
>
> Informal: Babulya
>
> Variations: Baboushka, Babouchka, Babooshka

A Grandmother by Any Other Name Is Still as Sweet

iStockphoto/Thinkstock

Slovakian: Babicka

Slovenian: Stara Mama

Spanish

> Formal: Abuela
>
> Informal: Abuelita
>
> Variations: Lita, Litta

Swedish

> Paternal: FarMor
>
> Maternal: MorMor

Swiss: Grossmami

Syrian: Teta, Jadda

Tamil: Pathi

Thai

> Maternal: Ya
>
> Paternal: Yai

Turkish: Buyuk Anne, Anneanne, Babanne

Turkmen: Ene

Ukranian

>Formal: Babusia

>Informal: Baba

Uzbek: Bibi

Vietnamese

>Formal: Danhtá

>Informal: Ba, Bégià

Welsh

>Southern: Mamgu

>Northern: Naini, Nain

VStock/Thinkstock

CHAPTER 3

That Special Bond

There's a Welsh proverb that goes, "Perfect love sometimes does not come until the first grandchild." Then there's Sam Levenson's contention that "the reason grandchildren and grandparents get along so well is that they have a common enemy." Like anything else in life, it's a matter of perspective.

• • •

"When you have a grandchild, you have two children."
—JEWISH PROVERB

• • •

"Grandparents, like heroes, are as necessary to a child's growth as vitamins."
—JOYCE ALLSTON

• • •

"The best babysitters, of course, are the baby's grandparents. You feel completely comfortable entrusting your baby to them for long periods, which is why most grandparents flee to Florida."
—DAVE BARRY

• • •

"Because [grandparents] are usually free to love and guide and befriend the young without having to take daily responsibility for them, they can often reach out past pride and fear of failure and close the space between generations."
—JIMMY CARTER

• • •

"Being grandparents sufficiently removes us from the responsibilities so that we can be friends."
—ALLAN FROMME

• • •

"It's impossible for a grandmother to understand that few people, and maybe none, will find her grandchild as endearing as she does."
—JANET LANESE

• • •

"Something magical happens when parents turns into grand-parents. Their attitude changes from 'money-doesn't-grow-on-trees' to spending it like it does."
—PAUL LINDEN

• • •

"They say genes skip generations. Maybe that's why grandparents find their grandchildren so likeable."
—JOAN MCINTOSH

• • •

"By the time the youngest children have learned to keep the house tidy, the oldest grandchildren are on hand to tear it to pieces."
—CHRISTOPHER MORLEY

• • •

"The feeling of grandparents for their grandchildren can be expressed this way: 'Our children are dear to us; but when we have grandchildren, they seem to be more dear than our children were.'"
—HENRY OLD COYOTE

• • •

"Grandmother grandchild relationships are simple. Grandmas are short on criticism and long on love."
—AUTHOR UNKNOWN

• • •

"Grandchildren are God's way of compensating us for growing old."
—MARY H. WALDRIP

• • •

VStock/Thinkstock

iStockphoto/Thinkstock

"Grandma and Grandpa, tell me a story and snuggle me with your love. When I'm in your arms, the world seems small and we're blessed by the heavens above."
—LAURA SPIESS

• • •

"Even young grandparents seem enormously old to a small child, although the child may politely deny it. One small girl, feeling proud of reaching the monumental age of four, turned to her young-looking grandmother and asked, 'How come I'm so old if you're so new?'"
—ALISON JUDSON RYERSON

• • •

"Elephants and grandchildren never forget."
—ANDY ROONEY

• • •

"The presence of a grandparent confirms that parents were, indeed, little once, too, and that people who are little can grow to be big, can become parents, and one day even have grandchildren of their own. So often we think of grandparents as belonging to the past; but in this important way, grandparents, for young children, belong to the future."
—FRED ROGERS

• • •

"Grandparents are similar to a piece of string—handy to have around and easily wrapped around the fingers of their grandchildren."
—AUTHOR UNKNOWN

• • •

"When grandparents enter the door, discipline flies out the window."
—OGDEN NASH

• • •

iStockphoto/Thinkstock

"The motherless child will suckle the grandmother."
—AFRICAN PROVERB

• • •

"It's so important to give your children and grandchildren inspiration . . . Teach them to notice, to pay attention, to appreciate, and to be inquisitive. Don't just look, try to see."
—IRINA BARONOVA-TENNANT

• • •

"If a child is to keep alive his inborn sense of wonder, he needs the companionship of at least one adult who can share it, rediscovering with him the joy, excitement, and mystery of the world we live in."
—RACHEL CARSON

• • •

"We find delight in the beauty and happiness of children that makes the heart too big for the body."
—RALPH WALDO EMERSON

• • •

iStockphoto/Thinkstock

"Our grandchildren accept us for ourselves, without rebuke or effort to change us, as no one in our entire lives has ever done, not our parents, siblings, spouses, friends—and hardly ever our own grown children."
—RUTH GOODE

• • •

"God gave us loving grandchildren as a reward for all our random acts of kindness."
—JANET LANESE

• • •

"A zest for life is one of the most important examples a grandparent can pass on to their grandchildren."
—AUTHOR UNKNOWN

• • •

"I loved their home. Everything smelled older, worn but safe; the food aroma had baked itself into the furniture."
—SUSAN STRASBERG

• • •

"Everyone needs to have access both to grandparents and grandchildren in order to be a full human being."
—MARGARET MEAD

• • •

"Posterity is the patriotic name for grandchildren."
—ART LINKLETTER

• • •

"The simplest toy, one which even the youngest child can operate, is called a grandparent."
—SAM LEVENSON

• • •

"Nobody can do for little children what grandparents do. Grandparents sort of sprinkle stardust over the lives of little children."
—ALEX HALEY

• • •

iStockphoto/Thinkstock

iStockphoto/Thinkstock

"The idea that no one is perfect is a view most commonly held by people with no grandchildren."
—DOUG LARSON

• • •

"The very fact that you don't look or act or feel like the grandparents of even a generation ago does not mean that you are less, but that you are more—in effect, an evolved form of grandparents, primed to do a bigger and more challenging job than any group before you."
—ARTHUR KORNHABER, M.D.

• • •

"In order not to influence a child, one must be careful not to be that child's parent or grandparent."
—DON MARQUIS

• • •

"Nothing you do for children is ever wasted."
—GARRISON KEILLOR

• • •

"If nothing is going well, call your grandmother."
—ITALIAN PROVERB

• • •

"Grandparents who want to be truly helpful will do well to
keep their mouths shut and their opinions to themselves until
these are requested."
—THOMAS BERRY BRAZELTON

• • •

"Being pretty on the inside means you don't hit your brother
and you eat all your peas—that's what my grandma taught me."
—LORD CHESTERFIELD

• • •

iStockphoto/Thinkstock

iStockphoto/Thinkstock

"So many people say they dream of doing a thing, but many times, they lack the courage to even try. Grandma provided that courage for me. And even though I haven't reached my goal yet, I know I will. And someday, I pray that some other little girl will lie in bed with her grandma, reading my books, and dare to dream all the possibilities for her life. Because with her grandma's help, she's sure to achieve them."
—DANICA FAVORITE

• • •

"The handwriting on the wall means the grandchildren found the crayons."
—AUTHOR UNKNOWN

• • •

"To show a child what has once delighted you, to find the child's delight added to your own, so that there is now a double delight seen in the glow of trust and affection, this is happiness."
—J. B. PRIESTLEY

• • •

"My great-grandfather used to say to his wife, my great-grand-mother, who in turn told her daughter, my grandmother, who repeated it to her daughter, my mother, who used to remind her daughter, my own sister, that to talk well and eloquently was a very great art, but that an equally great one was to know the right moment to stop."
—WOLFGANG AMADEUS MOZART

• • •

"One of life's greatest mysteries is how the boy who wasn't good enough to marry your daughter can be the father of the smartest grandchild in the world."
—JEWISH PROVERB

• • •

"Grandparents should play the same role in the family as an elder statesman can in the government of a country. They have the experience and knowledge that comes from surviving a great many years of life's battles and the wisdom, hopefully, to recognize how their grandchildren can benefit from this."
—GEOFF DENCH

• • •

iStockphoto/Thinkstock

iStockphoto/Thinkstock

"My grandmother would say, 'Make sure you look good. Make sure you speak well. Make sure you remain that Southern gentleman that I've taught you to be.'"
—JAMIE FOXX

• • •

"We must act as elders of the tribe, looking out for the interests of the future and preserving the precious compact between the generations."
—MAGGIE KUHN

• • •

"It would be more honorable to our distinguished ancestors to praise them in words less, but in deeds to imitate them more."
—HORACE MANN

• • •

"Grandchildren are the dots that connect the lines from generation to generation."
—LOIS WYSE

• • •

"No cowboy was ever faster on the draw than a grandparent
pulling a baby picture out of a wallet."
—AUTHOR UNKNOWN

• • •

"The birth of a grandchild is a wonderful and exciting event!
That wonder and excitement continues throughout life."
—TOM POTTS

• • •

"The secret of life is to skip having children and go directly to
grandchildren."
—MEL LAZARUS

• • •

"If I would have known that grandchildren were going to be
so much fun, I would have had them first."
—BILL LAURIN

• • •

iStockphoto/Thinkstock

"The history of our grandparents is remembered not with rose petals but in the laughter and tears of their children and their children's children. It is into us that the lives of grandparents have gone. It is in us that their history becomes a future."
—CHARLES AND ANN MORSE

• • •

"The closest friends I made all through life have been people who also grew up close to a loved and loving grandmother or grandfather."
—MARGARET MEAD

• • •

"There is a fountain of youth: it is your mind, your talents, the creativity you bring to your life and the lives of the people you love. When you learn to tap this source, you will have truly defeated age."
—SOPHIA LOREN

• • •

"What children need most are the essentials that grandparents provide in abundance. They give unconditional love, kindness, patience, humor, comfort, lessons in life. And, most importantly, cookies."
—RUDOLPH GIULIANI

• • •

"Few things are more delightful than grandchildren fighting over your lap."
—DOUG LARSON

• • •

"I don't intentionally spoil my grandkids. It's just that correcting them often takes more energy than I have left."
—GENE PERRET

• • •

"Although you've raised children of your own, now you don't have to worry about all the responsibilities that come with parenting. You've earned the right to enjoy being a grandparent."
—AUTHOR UNKNOWN

• • •

Comstock/Thinkstock

Chapter 4

Grandma's Playbook

You've been asked to babysit for a few hours or maybe even for a weekend. In between naps and snacktime, here are some ideas to keep the grandkids busy and have some fun yourself. The list of films at the end of the chapter provides a last resort for when you've run out of energy!

What to do if the weather's nice:

- Visit the cows at the local farm
- Take a hike
- Play tag
- Create a space in your vegetable or flower garden just for your grandchild
- Go sledding
- If you have access to a pool, play Marco Polo
- Catch fireflies
- Go on a scavenger hunt
- At the beach, let your grandchild bury you
- Make a daisy chain
- Have a snowball fight
- Build a fort out of cardboard boxes
- Play jacks or marbles
- Skip rope

What to do if the weather keeps you indoors:

- Read a book that you read to your grandchild's parent when he or she was young
- Make paper airplanes, paper dolls, or paper snowflakes
- Play Go Fish
- Bring our your favorite board games
- Create a collage of a trip you've taken together
- Visit the library
- Play pretend store
- Tell knock-knock jokes
- Make a terrarium
- Bake cookies or cupcakes
- Play hangman or tic-tac-toe
- Make a fort out of the sofa cushions
- Visit the nearest children's museum
- Teach your grandchild how to knit or sew
- Sing songs in the round
- Do a jigsaw puzzle together
- Carve pumpkins or make funny critters out of vegetables and toothpicks
- Play dress up
- Put on a mini play
- Play Simon Says

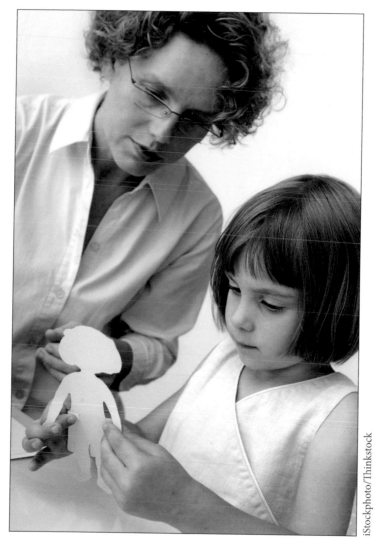

Some of the best children's books of all time:

For ages six months to three years:

Goodnight Moon by Margaret Wise Brown, illustrated by Clement Hurd

The Very Hungry Caterpillar by Eric Carle

The Snowy Day by Ezra Jack Keats

Chicka Chicka Boom Boom by Bill Martin Jr. and John Archambault, illustrated by Lois Ehlert

Caps for Sale by Esphyr Slobodkina

For ages three to six:

Where the Wild Things Are by Maurice Sendak

The Cat in the Hat by Dr. Seuss

Knuffle Bunny by Mo Willems

Madeline by Ludwig Bemelmans

The Complete Adventures of Curious George by H. A. and Margret Rey

The Tale of Peter Rabbit by Beatrix Potter

Bark, George by Jules Feiffer

Lilly's Purple Plastic Purse by Kevin Henkes

Hemera/Thinkstock

Creatas/© Getty Images/Thinkstock

George and Martha by James Marshall
The Paper Bag Princess by Robert Munsch, illustrated by Michael Martchenko
Olivia by Ian Falconer
Mufaro's Beautiful Daughters: An African Tale by John Steptoe
Are You My Mother? by P.D. Eastman
Little Bear by Else Holmelund Minarik, illustrated by Maurice Sendak
Doctor De Soto by William Steig
Go Away, Big Green Monster! by Ed Emberley

For ages six to nine:

Ramona the Pest by Beverly Cleary
Anna Hibiscus by Atinuke
Moonshot: The Flight of Apollo 11 by Brian Floca
Mirror Mirror: A Book of Reversible Verse by Marilyn Singer, illustrated by Josee Masse
Dave the Potter: Artist, Poet, Slave by Laban Carrick Hill, illustrated by Bryan Collier
My Father's Dragon by Ruth Gannett Stiles, illustrated by Ruth Chrisman Gannett

For ages eight to twelve:

Charlotte's Web by E. B. White
Harry Potter and the Sorcerer's Stone by J. K. Rowling
A Wrinkle in Time by Madeleine L'Engle
The Lion, the Witch and the Wardrobe by C. S. Lewis
The Secret Garden by Frances Hodgson Burnett
Harriet the Spy by Louise Fitzhugh
Charlie and the Chocolate Factory by Roald Dahl
The Hobbit by J. R. R. Tolkien
The Phantom Tollbooth by Norton Juster
Holes by Louis Sachar
The Arrival by Shaun Tan
Matilda by Roald Dahl
The Invention of Hugo Cabret by Brian Selznick
A Light in the Attic by Shel Silverstein
Tales of a Fourth Grade Nothing by Judy Blume
The Watsons Go to Birmingham—1963 by Christopher Paul Curtis
From the Mixed-Up Files of Mrs. Basil E. Frankweiler by E. L. Konigsburg
Coraline by Neil Gaiman
The Bone series by Jeff Smith
The Golden Compass by Philip Pullman
Esperanza Rising by Pam Muñoz Ryan
Amelia Lost by Candace Fleming

• • •

"Love was exactly what my grandmother had been giving me all of my years. She resisted the happiness of a beaming child opening an expensive toy and replaced it with a gift that was a part of her. She didn't give me what I wanted in my little girl mind, but what she knew I needed—a gift for the soul that would last a lifetime. Now I saw how wise she had been and how each book was so carefully selected at different times of my life."
—Elizabeth Rose Reardon Farella

• • •

Knock-knock jokes:

Knock knock.
Who's there?
Cash.
Cash who?
No thanks, but I would like a peanut instead!

• • •

Knock knock.
Who's there?
Banana.
Banana who?
Knock knock.
Who's there?
Banana.
Banana who?
Knock knock.
Who's there?
Banana.
Banana who?
Knock knock.
Who's there?
Orange.
Orange who?
Orange you glad I didn't say "banana"?

• • •

Photos.com/© Getty Images/Thinkstock

Knock knock.
Who's there?
Interrupting cow.
Interrup . . .
Mooooooooooooooo!!

• • •

Knock knock.
Who's there?
Honey bee.
Honey bee who?
Honey bee a dear and get me a soda!

• • •

Knock knock?
Who's there?
Me.
Me who?
No, seriously, it's just me. I am telling a knock-knock joke.

• • •

Knock, knock.
Who's there?
Nana.
Nana who?
Nana your business.

• • •

Knock knock.
Who's there?
Oink oink.
Oink oink who?
Make up your mind, are you a pig or an owl?!

• • •

Knock knock.
Who's there?
Ya.
Ya who?
Wow. You sure are excited to see me!

• • •

Knock knock.
Who's there?
Cows go.
Cows go who?
Cows don't go who, they go moo!

• • •

Knock knock.
Who's there?
Arfur.
Arfur who?
Arfur got!

• • •

Blend Images/Thinkstock

iStockphoto/Thinkstock

Knock knock.
Who's there?
Etch.
Etch who?
Bless you!

• • •

Knock knock.
Who's there?
Canoe.
Canoe who?
Canoe help me with my homework?

• • •

Knock knock.
Who's there?
Claire.
Claire who?
Claire the way, I'm coming through!

• • •

iStockphoto/ThinkStock

Grandma's Playbook

Knock knock.
Who's there?
Harry.
Harry who?
Harry up, it's cold out here!

• • •

Knock knock.
Who's there?
A herd.
A herd who?
A herd you were home, so I came over!

• • •

Knock knock.
Who's there?
Adore.
Adore who?
Adore is between us. Open up!

• • •

Knock knock.
Who's there?
Otto.
Otto who?
Otto know. I've got amnesia.

• • •

iStockphoto/Thinkstock

Knock knock.
Who's there?
Dwayne.
Dwayne who?
Dwayne the bathtub. It's overflowing!

• • •

Knock knock.
Who's there?
Roach.
Roach who?
Roach you a letter, did you get it?

• • •

Knock knock.
Who's there?
Aida.
Aida who?
Aida sandwich for lunch today.

• • •

Knock knock.
Who's there?
Iona.
Iona who?
Iona new car!

• • •

Digital Vision/Thinkstock

Songs kids love:

"The Farmer in the Dell"
"Old MacDonald Had a Farm"
"Five Little Monkeys Swinging in the Tree"
"Frère Jacques"
"Itsy Bitsy Spider"
"Miss Mary Mack"
"On Top of Spaghetti"
"Twinkle, Twinkle, Little Star"
"The Wheels on the Bus"
"This Old Man"
"Are You Sleeping?"
"Bingo"
"Hokey Pokey"
"The Alphabet Song"
"It's Raining, It's Pouring"
"Shoo Fly, Don't Bother Me"
"London Bridge"
"I See the Moon"

Songs about grandmothers:

"Be-Bop Grandma" by The Destroyers (1999)

"Grandma" by The Moffatts (1995)

"Grandma Drove a Buick" by Jill King (2008)

"Grandma Harp" by Merle Haggard (1972)

"Grandma's Big Ol' Buick" by Chris McGlothlin (2009)

"Grandma's Hands" by Jeff Lorber (2007)

"Grandma's House" by Chris Kenner (1956)

"Grandma's Old Wood Stove" by The Sanders (1989)

"Grandma's Song" by Gail Davies (1981)

"Granny" by Cat Stevens (1967)

"Hey, Grandma" by Moby Grape (1967)

"Hootenanny Granny" by Jim Lowe (1963)

"Rockin' and Rollin' with Grandma" by Carson Robison (1956)

iStockphoto/Thinkstock

Movies to enjoy with your grandchildren:

Bambi
Miracle on 34th Street
Little Fugitive
National Velvet
Alice in Wonderland
Old Yeller
Meet Me in St. Louis
The 5,000 Fingers of Dr. T
Bright Eyes
Curse of the Cat People
The Seventh Voyage of Sinbad
Willy Wonka and the Chocolate Factory
Mary Poppins
The Sound of Music
Star Wars
The Black Stallion
The Muppet Movie
Snow White and the Seven Dwarfs
The Red Balloon
The Wizard of Oz

iStockphoto/Thinkstock

CHAPTER 5

Out of the Mouths of Babes . . .
and Grandmothers

In addition to sharing a common enemy, grandparents and grandchildren are also known to say the darnedest things. Children do this because they haven't yet learned all the nuances of social interaction, and older folks . . . well, because they just don't give a darn any more. Here are some jokes that grandmothers in particular will appreciate.

• • •

A little girl is watching her mother in the kitchen. She notices some strands of her mother's hair are turning white. "Mom," she asks, "why is some of your hair turning white?"

Annoyed, her mother responds, "Because I have a little girl who is constantly making trouble and causing me to worry."

The little girl thinks about it for a few minutes and says, "Mom, so why is Grandma's hair all white?"

• • •

Granddaughter: Grandma, were you on Noah's Ark?
Grandmother: No.
Granddaughter: Well, how did you survive the flood?

• • •

An elderly woman and her little grandson, whose face was sprinkled with bright freckles, spent the day at the zoo. Lots of children were waiting in line to get their cheeks painted by a local artist who was decorating them with tiger paws. "You've got so many freckles, there's no place to paint!" a girl in the line said to the little fella.

Embarrassed, the little boy dropped his head. His grandmother knelt down next to him. "I love your freckles. When I was a little girl, I always wanted freckles," she said while tracing her finger across the child's cheek. "Freckles are beautiful."

The boy looked up and said, "Really?"

"Of course," said the grandmother. "Why, just name me one thing that's prettier than freckles."

The little boy thought for a moment, peered intensely into his grandma's face, and softly whispered, "Wrinkles."

For two solid hours, the lady sitting next to a man on an airplane had told him about her grandchildren. She had even produced a plastic foldout photo album of all nine of the children. She finally realized that she had dominated the entire conversation. "Oh, I've done all the talking, and I'm so sorry. I know you certainly have something to say. Please, tell me . . . what do you think of my grandchildren?"

• • •

A grandmother was telling her little granddaughter what her own childhood was like: "We used to skate outside on a pond. I had a swing made from a tire; it hung from a tree in our front yard. We rode our pony. We picked wild raspberries in the woods."

The little girl was wide-eyed, taking this in. At last she said, "I sure wish I'd gotten to know you sooner!"

• • •

There was a virgin who was going out on a date for the first time and she told her grandmother about it.

Her grandmother said, "Sit here and let me tell you about those young boys. He is going to try to kiss you; you are going to like that, but don't let him do that." She continued, "He is going to try to feel your breast; you are going to like that, but don't let him do that. He is going to try to put his hand between your legs; you are going to like that, but don't let him do that." Then the grandmother said, "But, most importantly, he is going to try to get on top of you and have his way with you. You are going to like that, but don't let him do that. It will disgrace the family."

With that bit of advice in mind, the granddaughter went on her date and could not wait to tell her grandmother about it. The next day she told her grandmother that her date went just as the old lady said. She said, "Grandmother, I didn't let him disgrace the family. When he tried, I turned him over, got on top of him, and disgraced *his* family."

Ingram Publishing/Thinkstock

A little girl was sitting on her grandmother's lap as she read her a book. She repeatedly touched her grandmother's cheek and then her own, fascinated by the difference. "Grandma," she asked. "Did God make you?"

"Yes, dear," Grandma replied. "God made me a long time ago."

"Did God make me?" she asked.

"Yes, God made you too," answered Grandma.

"Well, he sure has gotten better over the years, hasn't he?"

• • •

A grandmother didn't know that her granddaughter had learned her colors, so she decided to test her. The grandmother would point out something and ask her grandchild what color it was.

After a few rounds of this, the granddaughter said, "Grandma, I think you should try to figure out some of these yourself!"

• • •

A grandson was visiting his grandmother one day when he asked, "Gramma, do you know how you and God are alike?"

The grandmother mentally polished her halo and asked, "No, how are we alike?"

"You're both old," he replied.

• • •

A grandmother was surprised by her seven-year-old grandson one morning. He had made her coffee. She drank what was possibly the worst cup of coffee in her life. When she got to the bottom of the cup, there were three of those little green army men, and she asked him why they were there.

Her grandson replied, "On television they say, 'The best part of waking up is soldiers in your cup!'"

• • •

iStockphoto/Thinkstock

James Woodson/Digital Vision/Thinkstock

A little boy asked his grandmother what year she was born.

She told him she was born in 1935.

"Wow!" the boy exclaimed. "If you were a baseball card, you'd be worth lots of money."

• • •

When a three-year-old boy opened a birthday gift from his grandmother, he discovered a water pistol. He squealed with delight and headed for the nearest sink. His mother was not so pleased and she said to the grandmother, "Mom, I'm surprised at you. Don't you remember how we used to drive you crazy with water guns?"

The grandmother smiled and then replied, "I remember . . ."

• • •

A granddaughter came to spend a few weeks with her grandmother, who had decided to teach her to sew. After Grandma had gone through a lengthy explanation of how to thread the machine, the granddaughter stepped back, put her hands on her hips, and said in disbelief, "You mean you can do all that, but you can't play my Game Boy?"

• • •

A Jewish grandmother was giving directions to her grown grandson who was coming to visit with his wife: "You come to the front door of the apartment complex. I am in apartment 14T. There is a big panel at the door. With your elbow, push button 14T. I will buzz you in. Come inside, the elevator is on the right. Get in, and with your elbow hit 14. When you get out I am on the left. With your elbow, hit my doorbell."

"Grandma, that sounds easy, but why am I hitting all these buttons with my elbow?"

"You're coming empty handed?"

• • •

A young boy and his doting grandmother were walking along the sea shore when a huge wave appeared out of nowhere, sweeping the child out to sea. The horrified woman fell to her knees, raised her eyes to the heavens, and begged the Lord to return her beloved grandson. And, another wave reared up and deposited the stunned child on the sand. The grandmother looked the boy over carefully. He was fine. But still she stared up angrily toward the heavens. "When we came," she snapped indignantly, "he had a hat!"

• • •

When the school bus driver stopped to pick up Chris for preschool, he noticed an older woman hugging him. "Is that your grandmother?" the driver asked.

"Yes," Chris said. "She's come to visit us for Christmas."

"How nice," the driver said. "Where does she live?"

"At the airport," Chris replied. "Whenever we want her, we just go out there and get her."

• • •

Little Tony was so happy to see his grandmother that he ran up and gave her a big hug. "I'm so happy to see you, Grandma. Now Daddy will have to do that trick he's been promising to do!"

His grandmother was curious. "What trick is that, sweetie?"

The little guy grinned at her. "I heard Daddy tell Mommy that he would climb the gosh-darn walls if you came to visit us again!"

• • •

A little boy went to the store with his grandmother and on the way home, he was looking at the things she had purchased. He found a package of panty hose and began to sound out the words "Queen Size." He then turned to his grandmother and exclaimed, "Look Grandma, you wear the same size as our bed!"

• • •

A second grader came home from school and said to her grandmother, "Grandma, guess what. We learned how to make babies today."

The grandmother, more than a little surprised, tried to keep her cool. "That's interesting," she said. "How do you make babies?"

"It's simple," replied the girl. "You just change 'y' to 'i' and add 'es.'"

• • •

iStockphoto/Thinkstock

After putting her grandchildren to bed, a grandmother changed into old slacks and a droopy blouse and proceeded to wash her hair. As she heard the children getting more and more rambunctious, her patience grew thin. Finally, she threw a towel around her head and stormed into their room, putting them back to bed with stern warnings. As she left the room, she heard the three-year-old say with a trembling voice, "Who was *that*?"

• • •

A grandmother was in the bathroom, putting on her makeup, under the watchful eyes of her young granddaughter, as she'd done many times before. After she applied her lipstick and started to leave, the little one said, "But Gramma, you forgot to kiss the toilet paper good-bye!"

• • •

When a little boy asked his grandmother how old she was, she teasingly replied, "I'm not sure."

"Look in your underwear," he suggested. "Mine says I'm four to six."

• • •

A little girl was diligently pounding away on her grandmother's computer. She told Grandma she was writing a story.

"What's it about?" Grandma asked.

"I don't know," the girl replied. "I can't read."

• • •

A grandson called to wish his grandmother a happy birthday. He asked her how old she was.

When she told him she was sixty-two, he got quiet for a moment and then asked, "Did you start at one?"

• • •

iStockphoto/Thinkstock

Chapter 6

Poems That Celebrate Grandmotherhood

With all her beauty, wisdom, and power, a grandmother makes a fitting subject for poetry. The following poems reveal the universal affection that she has inspired throughout the ages.

• • •

Grandmother

Grandmother, you are like a patchwork quilt
So cozy and warm.
Just the smell of coffee
Reminds me of your wisdom and charm.

I know I can always come to you
When lost or alone.
For you always comfort me
And make me feel at home.

You are the silver lining of a cloudy day.
And I know whom I can trust
when clouds blow my way.
Grandmother, your hugs and kisses
Will be stored in my heart each day.
—AUTHOR UNKNOWN

What Are Grandmas For

Grandmas are for stories
about things of long ago.
Grandmas are for caring
about all the things you know . . .
Grandmas are for rocking you
and singing you to sleep,
Grandmas are for giving you
nice memories to keep . . .
Grandmas are for knowing
all the things you're dreaming of . . .
But, most importantly of all,
Grandmas are for love.
—AUTHOR UNKNOWN

credit: iStockphoto/Thinkstock

We'd Wish Our Kids Were Small Again . . .

If we were granted any wish, I'll tell you what we'd do,
We'd wish our kids were small again, for just a month or two.
To hear their squeals of laughter, to watch them while they
play.
And when they ask us to join in, we wouldn't say, "Not today."

To hug again their chubby frames, to kiss away their tears,
and cherish childhood innocence that washed away the years.
Then when it's story time again, we'd stay a little longer,
to answer questions, sing the songs, so memories would be
stronger.

But time is callous, wishes, myth, yet God in all his wisdom,
has given us another chance before we join his kingdom.
Your faces may not be just the same, your names are changed,
'tis true,
but yet the smile that radiates, reminds us so much of you.

God must have known that grandparents would need a
chance or two.
For many little happy things we hadn't time to do.
So God gave love to grandparents to equal that before,
that in effect embraces those little lives they bore.
—AUTHOR UNKNOWN

The Joys of Being a Grandparent

Telling stories, buying ice cream, playing silly games,
Hugging, kissing, tickling, giggling, making up fun names.
Going fishing, baby-sitting, tucking in at night,
Dreaming, reading, make-believing, holding hands real tight.
Having picnics, watching movies, buying toys and things—
These are just a few of the joys that being a grandparent
brings!
—AUTHOR UNKNOWN

• • •

Grandkids

I've seen the lights of Paris
I've seen the lights of Rome
But the greatest lights I've ever seen
Are the tail lights of my children's car
Taking my grandkids home.
—AUTHOR UNKNOWN

GrandChild

Child of my child,
Heart of my heart,
Your smile bridges the years between us—
I am young again discovering the world
through your eyes.
You have the time to listen
And I have the time to spend.
Delighted to gaze at familiar,
loved features, made new in you again.
Through you, I'll see the future
Through me, you'll know the past
In the present we'll love one another
As long as these moments last.
—AUTHOR UNKNOWN

Motherhood's Reward

She rocks another baby . . .
hums an age-old lullaby.
She hopes no one is watching
as with thanks, she starts to cry.

Remembering the time
when the babies were her own,
And her mother told her gently
too soon they would be grown.

Lots of bedtime stories,
skinned knees, and tears to dry,
Teddy bears, toy trucks and dolls
and kites up in the sky.

First days of school, first loves, first cars,
the proms, the wedding days,
Sand castles and snowball fights
and teaching them to pray.
Now, as she holds her grandchild
and gives thanks unto the Lord,
She knows to be a grandma
is motherhood's reward!
—AUTHOR UNKNOWN

CHAPTER 7

Brought Up by Grandma

According to the 2010 US Census, about seven percent of children under eighteen are living with their grandparents, and, in many cases, are being raised by them. What follows are remembrances by several famous Americans who count their grandmothers as especially strong influences in their lives.

• • •

"I knew all sorts of things about her that only I knew because we slept in the same bed. I don't have that closeness with my grandsons nor with the little ones. But they have parents. My mother and father for all intents and purposes abandoned my brother and me when we were three and five. My grandmother was the best. She didn't talk much. She spoke very softly when she did, although she had truly a huge voice; when she sang in church the windows would rattle."
—POET MAYA ANGELOU

"Mammaw's main goals for me were that I would eat a lot, learn a lot, and always be neat and clean. We ate in the kitchen at a table next to the window. My high chair faced the window, and Mammaw tacked playing cards up on the wooden window frame at mealtimes so that I could learn to count. She also stuffed me at every meal, because conventional wisdom at the time was that a fat baby was a healthy one, as long as he bathed every day. At least once a day, she read to me from *Dick and Jane* books until I could read them myself, and from *World Book Encyclopedia* volumes. . . . These early instructions probably explain why I now read a lot, love card games, battle my weight, and never forget to wash my hands and brush my teeth."

—PRESIDENT BILL CLINTON, FROM HIS
AUTOBIOGRAPHY, *MY LIFE*

credit: iStockphoto/Thinkstock

credit: Zoonar/Thinkstock

"Rose was petite with dark hair and sharp, delicate features, with a characteristic pointed nose, 'the Mitchell nose,' as it was known in the family and which was inherited from her father, Jack Mitchell. Photographs of her as a young woman show her to have been very pretty, quite the beauty among her sisters. But at some point at the outset of the war, when she had just turned thirty, she underwent surgery for a serious problem with her palette. During the operation there was a power cut that resulted in the surgery having to be abandoned, leaving her with a massive scar underneath her left cheekbone that gave the impression that a piece of her cheek had been hollowed out. This left her with a certain amount of self-consciousness. In his song 'Not Dark Yet,' Dylan wrote, 'Behind every beautiful face there's been some kind of pain.' Her suffering made her a very warm person with a deep compassion for other people's dilemmas. She was the focus of my life for much of my upbringing."
—MUSICIAN ERIC CLAPTON, FROM HIS
AUTOBIOGRAPHY, *CLAPTON*

"So I lived with my grandparents and with an aunt and an uncle in a lodging house which was glorious. I used to sleep upstairs with the lodgers. It was great. I was happy, so there was love within all of that."
—ACTOR PIERCE BROSNAN

• • •

"I made [my grandmother] a promise in 1988 that I would take care of her after her husband died, and I did until she passed away. I wish I would have told her there was nobody that loved her more, or anybody that would have protected her more than me."
—COMEDIAN GEORGE LOPEZ

• • •

"She was the cornerstone of our family, and a woman of extraordinary accomplishment, strength, and humility. She was the person who encouraged and allowed us to take chances."
—PRESIDENT BARACK OBAMA

credit: iStockphoto/Thinkstock

Brought Up by Grandma

"I vividly remember standing on my grandmother's small screened-in back porch, churning butter while she boiled clothes in a big black cast-iron pot in the yard. As she pulled the steaming clothes from the pot to hang on the line to dry, she called to me, 'Oprah Gail, you better watch me now, 'cause one day you gon' have to know how to do this for yourself.'

I did what she told me. I watched carefully as she pulled the clothespins from her apron, held them two at a time between her lips, and placed one and then the other on opposite ends of the sheets and towels and shirts and dresses she hung on the line.

A still, small voice inside me, really more a feeling than a voice, said, 'This will not be your life. Your life will be more than hanging clothes on a line.'"

—OPRAH WINFREY

"There had been a serious family conference after Daddy Nelson's funeral about who we should live with. Bobbie and I didn't want to leave Mama Nelson. We did not want to be anywhere else and we refused to be split up. We'd been with our grandmother all our lives. She lived and breathed for us, worked for us, gave us her undivided attention. We were allowed to stay in our little home with her, and we were happy."
—MUSICIAN WILLIE NELSON, FROM HIS AUTOBIOGRAPHY, *WILLIE*

• • •

"They never told me, 'You can be whatever you want to be.' I think that's a great lie, a horrible lie. But they told me to try, have a right go for it, see what happens. It was always just a bit practical. I think I'm quite a practical person as a result."
—ACTOR JAMES MCAVOY

• • •

"Show me any woman today who could keep a secret, confidence, or an intimacy to that degree. You got my kind of gal."
—JACK NICHOLSON

credit: iStockphoto/Thinkstock

credit: iStockphoto/Thinkstock

"My grandmother Nanny and I were at the picture show.
I hadn't reached two digits yet in age because I distinctly
remember my feet couldn't touch the floor of the movie
house. Nanny and I were still living in San Antonio, Texas.
My mama and daddy had gone ahead to California, where
Nanny and I would later wind up. The feature had just begun,
and his [Jimmy Stewart's] face lit up the screen. I couldn't
take my eyes off him. He was talking to a beautiful lady in
a nightclub somewhere. I'm not sure what the movie was. It
didn't matter. He had a kind of crooked smile and spoke with
a soft . . . what kind of voice was it? A *drawl*? The camera
followed him as he stood up. You could see how very long his
legs were. I was sure *his* feet never had trouble reaching the
floor. 'Skinny as a string bean,' Nanny said. After the picture
show, we went home to the old house, and I couldn't get the
man in the movie out of my mind. He wasn't just an actor
like all the others I'd seen in picture shows. This man was
different. *He spoke to me.* I tried to explain this to Nanny.

'Nanny, I know that man.'

'What do you mean, you know him?'

'I just do. He's my friend; we just haven't met yet.'

'That's nice, dear. Drink your Ovaltine and go to bed.'"

—CAROL BURNETT IN HER AUTOBIOGRAPHY,
THIS TIME TOGETHER

A Few Famous Grandmothers:

Martha Stewart – became a grandmother on March 8, 2011
Kris Jenner – became a grandmother on December 14, 2009
Sarah Palin – became a grandmother in late 2008 (her son, Trig, was born in April 2008).
Goldie Hawn – became a grandmother in 2004
Joan Rivers – became a grandmother in 2000 (her grandson calls her "Nana New Face")
Blythe Danner – became a grandmother in 2004
Nancy Pelosi – is the grandmother of eight.
Whoopi Goldberg – became a grandmother at age thirty-four
Priscilla Presley – became a grandmother in 1989
Katherine Jackson – became a great-grandmother in 2000
Naomi Judd – became a grandmother in 1994
Marian Robinson – mother of Michelle Obama and grandmother to Malia and Sasha

credit: iStockphoto/Thinkstock

credit: Wavebreak Media/ThinkStock

Chapter 8

Staying Young in Mind, Heart, and Spirit

Now that you've got grandchildren, they'll expect you to stay physically and mentally active no matter how much your back hurts or how much you'd rather take a nap. Here's some advice that might alter your perspective on getting older.

• • •

"It would help not to treat age as if it were any less of a pleasure than it was when we were six and saying, 'I'm six and a half.' You know, we could be saying, 'I'm fifty and a half' and say it with joy. Each age is different and has different discoveries and pleasures."
—GLORIA STEINEM

• • •

"Age is an issue of mind over matter. If you don't mind, it doesn't matter."
—MARK TWAIN

• • •

"Aging is not lost youth but a new stage of opportunity and strength."
—BETTY FRIEDAN

• • •

"Well, I don't like getting older; I have to tell you that. . . . But I think that what I have loved in my life are the intergenerational activities. . . . I have always enjoyed having people of different ages around me. I have thought that was fun. I do think that one needs to have respect for people who are older. I really do love the idea that one can respect generations."
—MADELEINE ALBRIGHT

• • •

"To keep the heart unwrinkled, to be hopeful, kindly, cheerful, reverent—that is to triumph over old age."
—THOMAS BAILEY ALDRICH

• • •

"We are not victims of aging, sickness, and death. These are part of scenery, not the seer, who is immune to any form of change. This seer is the spirit, the expression of eternal being."
—DEEPAK CHOPRA

• • •

"If I'd known I was going to live this long, I'd have taken better care of myself."
—EUBIE BLAKE

• • •

"Growing old is mandatory; growing up is optional."
—CHILI DAVIS

• • •

"We don't stop playing because we grow old. We grow old
because we stop playing."
—GEORGE BERNARD SHAW

• • •

"How old would you be if you didn't know how old you are?"
—SATCHEL PAIGE

• • •

"Old age is no place for sissies."
—BETTE DAVIS

• • •

"I think the main problem people have getting older, whether they know it or not, is that you're closer to dying. We may fixate on not wanting to look a certain way, but it really is just the clock ticking, that it means, 'Oh, I am not immortal!' Instead of fixating on the physical aspects of aging, it's good to contemplate the deeper source of our anxiety. That can be liberating. . . . I am so much happier and contented and less agitated; I'm just calmer. So it's like everything in this human existence: it's a trade-off. It's like you trade the virility of the body for the agility of the spirit."
—ELIZABETH LESSER

• • •

"Beautiful young people are accidents of nature, but beautiful old people are works of art."
—ELEANOR ROOSEVELT

• • •

"The great secret that all old people share is that you really haven't changed in seventy or eighty years. Your body changes, but you don't change at all."
—DORIS LESSING

• • •

credit: iStockphoto/Thinkstock

credit: Wavebreak Media/Thinkstock

"There's always a lot to be thankful for if you take time to look for it. For example, I am sitting here thinking how nice it is that wrinkles don't hurt."
—AUTHOR UNKNOWN

• • •

"The best part about being my age is in knowing how my life worked out."
—SCOTT ADAMS

• • •

"Those who love deeply never grow old; they may die of old age, but they die young."
—BEN FRANKLIN

• • •

"Grow old along with me! The best is yet to be, The last of life, for which the first was made: Our times are in his hands Who sayeth 'a whole I planned, Youth shows but half; Trust God; see all nor be afraid.'"
—ROBERT BROWNING

• • •

"We are redefining every age of our lives. All of us are. I mean twenty-year-olds today, they aren't where I was at twenty, and they're in a very different world. So how can we say that we're not different, we're not a different kind of sixty- or seventy- or eighty-year-old? We are! So I'm just hoping for myself and for the women around me and that I come into contact with, I just hope that I'm still learning. As long as I'm learning every day of my life, I will never feel old. Never. And I don't feel old; I feel in my head and in my heart, I don't know, ageless! That's I think because I'm still learning and still growing as a person."
—PAT MITCHELL

• • •

"Aging is an inevitable process. I surely wouldn't want to grow younger. The older you become, the more you know; your bank account of knowledge is much richer."
—WILLIAM HOLDEN

• • •

credit: iStockphoto/Thinkstock

credit: iStockphoto/Thinkstock

"I advise you to go on living solely to enrage those who are paying your annuities. It is the only pleasure I have left."
—VOLTAIRE

• • •

"Nothing is inherently and invincibly young except spirit. And spirit can enter a human being perhaps better in the quiet of old age and dwell there more undisturbed than in the turmoil of adventure."
—GEORGE SANTAYANA

• • •

"It's never too late to have a fling / For autumn is just as nice as spring / And it's never too late to fall in love."
—SANDY WILSON

• • •

"For the unlearned, old age is winter; for the learned, it is the season of the harvest."
—HASIDIC SAYING

• • •

"The reason that they make us all youth-oriented and vain and try to think that if we get old we are of no use anymore is because we get wiser, and they know that. And when I say 'they' I mean those who are fearful of change. We are getting older, and we are getting wiser, and we are getting freer. And when you get the wisdom and the truth, then you get the freedom and you get power, and then look out. Look out."
—MELISSA ETHERIDGE

• • •

"I think we need to very intentionally have women friends, and we need to seek out women who are braver, who challenge us, who can teach us, and who together with them we can face age with more courage."
—JANE FONDA

• • •

"[Aging] is an unfortunate thing that happens. I mean, yes, you can have millions of face lifts and all these different things that women have done to their bodies. . . . But personally (a) I haven't got the money for that, (b) I haven't got the time for it, and (c) there are more important things to me than how you look. I think the most important thing is to keep active and to hope that your mind stays active."
—JANE GOODALL

credit: VStock/Thinkstock

CHAPTER 9

Words of Wisdom for Great Women by Great Women

We rely on our elders—especially our grandmothers—to be the fonts of wisdom and sound advice. Whether you're of the mind that the best advice is no advice at all, or whether you dispense it without provocation, you'll no doubt find inspiration for yourself and your kin from the other sage women gathered here.

• • •

"My grandmother told me to be nice to everyone and always think about how you would feel if you were in their shoes. It's really good advice."
—AUTHOR UNKNOWN

• • •

"My gran had always told me that a woman—any woman worth her salt—could do whatever she had to."
—CHARLAINE HARRIS

• • •

"There is a special place in hell for women who don't help other women."
—MADELEINE ALBRIGHT

• • •

"If you meet a woman of whatever complexion who sails
through her life with strength and grace and assurance,
talk to her!"
—SENA JETER NASLUND

• • •

"There are women who make things better . . . simply by
showing up. There are women who make things happen.
There are women who make their way. There are
women who make a difference. And women who make us
smile. There are women of wit and wisdom who—
through strength and courage—make it through.
There are women who change the world everyday . . .
Women like you."
—ASHLEY RICE

• • •

"Do not stop thinking of life as an adventure.
You have no security unless you can live bravely,
excitingly, imaginatively; unless you can choose
a challenge instead of competence."
—ELEANOR ROOSEVELT

• • •

Barbara Penoyar/Photodisc/Thinkstock

iStockphoto/Thinkstock

"If we don't change, we don't grow. If we don't grow,
we are not really living. Growth demands a
temporary surrender of security."
—GAIL SHEEHY

• • •

"If you look at what you have in life, you'll always have
more. If you look at what you don't have in life, you'll
never have enough."
—OPRAH WINFREY

• • •

"Our deepest wishes are whispers of our authentic selves.
We must learn to respect them. We must learn to listen."
—SARAH BAN BREATHNACH

• • •

"Womanhood is a wonderful thing. In womankind we find the mothers of the race. There is no man so great, nor none sunk so low, but once he lay a helpless, innocent babe in a woman's arms and was dependent on her love and care for his existence. It is woman who rocks the cradle of the world and holds the first affections of mankind. She possesses a power beyond that of a king on his throne. . . . Womanhood stands for all that is pure and clean and noble. She who does not make the world better for having lived in it has failed to be all that a woman should be."
—MABEL HALE

• • •

"No matter what happened yesterday it is insignificant when compared to what lies within the core of your being today."
—SANDY BREWER

• • •

Hemera/Thinkstock

"The fact that I was a girl never damaged my ambitions
to be a pope or an emperor."
—WILLA CATHER

• • •

"Women want men, careers, money, children,
friends, luxury, comfort, independence, freedom,
respect, love, and a three-dollar pantyhose
that won't run."
—PHYLLIS DILLER

• • •

"When I dare to be powerful, to use my strength in the
service of my vision, then it becomes less and less
important whether I am afraid."
—AUDRE LORDE

• • •

"Above all, be the heroine of your life, not the victim."
—NORA EPHRON

• • •

"Well-behaved women seldom make history."
—LAUREL THATCHER ULRICH

• • •

"The thing women have yet to learn is nobody gives
you power. You just take it. "
—ROSEANNE BARR

• • •

"When a woman becomes her own best
friend life is easier."
—DIANE VON FURSTENBERG

• • •

"A girl should be two things: classy and fabulous."
—COCO CHANEL

• • •

Andrea Stanton Photography

"Grandma told me that every woman holds a vision of herself in her heart. 'You have to decide on the things you want in life and address them before you can commit to someone else,' she said. This piece of advice was the most shocking, because I thought she'd tell me the energy I'd invested in my career, my travels and my evolved world view were selfish endeavors. Instead, she applauded me for sowing my wild oats—and shaping myself into an interesting, self-knowing woman—before settling down with a man. She said that when I met the right guy, my sense of self-knowing wouldn't chase him away, but would rather make him love me even more."
—KRISTINE GASBARRE

• • •

"We're connected, as women. It's like a spiderweb. If one part of that web vibrates, if there's trouble, we all know it, but most of the time we're just too scared, or selfish, or insecure to help. But if we don't help each other, who will?"
—SARAH ADDISON ALLEN

• • •

"We never know how high we are
Till we are called to rise;
And then, if we are true to plan,
Our statures touch the skies."
—EMILY DICKINSON

• • •

"Dreams are necessary to life."
—ANAIS NIN

• • •

"You can learn new things at any time in your life if
you're willing to be a beginner. If you actually
learn to like being a beginner, the whole world
opens up to you."
—BARBARA SHER

• • •

Words of Wisdom for Great Women by Great Women

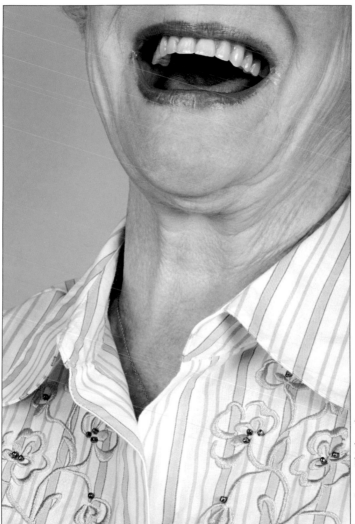

"If you knew what was going to happen, if you knew
everything that was going to happen next—if you
knew in advance the consequences of your own actions—
you'd be doomed. You'd be ruined as God. You'd be
a stone. You'd never eat or drink or laugh or get out
of bed in the morning. You'd never love anyone,
ever again. You'd never dare to."
—MARGARET ATWOOD

• • •

"The strength of a woman is not measured by the
impact that all her hardships in life have had on her;
but the strength of a woman is measured by the extent
of her refusal to allow those hardships to dictate
her and who she becomes."
—C. JOYBELL C.

• • •

"Okay, take a deep breath, I told myself. Don't go all hor-
monal. Get the facts straight. Have a mental doughnut."
—JANET EVANOVICH

• • •

"She looked like autumn, when leaves turned and
fruit ripened."
—SARAH ADDISON ALLEN

• • •

"Time and trouble will tame an advanced young
woman, but an advanced old woman is uncontrollable
by any earthly force."
—DOROTHY L. SAYERS

• • •

"In politics, if you want anything said, ask a man.
If you want anything done, ask a woman."
—MARGARET THATCHER

• • •

"The most damaging phrase in the language is:
'It's always been done that way.'"
—REAR ADMIRAL GRACE HOPPER

• • •

iStockphoto/Thinkstock

iStockphoto/Thinkstock

"The soul always knows what to do to heal itself.
The challenge is to silence the mind."
—CAROLINE MYSS

• • •

"It's never too late . . . never too late to start over,
never too late to be happy."
—JANE FONDA

• • •

"I've learned from experience that the greater part of our
happiness or misery depends on our dispositions
and not on our circumstances."
—MARTHA WASHINGTON

• • •

"It's not what you do once in a while, it's what you do
day in and day out that makes the difference."
—JENNY CRAIG

• • •

"Remember no one can make you feel inferior
without your consent."
—ELEANOR ROOSEVELT

• • •

"The most common way people give up their power
is by thinking they don't have any."
—ALICE WALKER

• • •

"Courage is like a muscle. We strengthen it with use."
—RUTH GORDON

• • •

"Better to be strong than pretty and useless."
—LILITH SAINTCROW

• • •

Jupiterimages/Brand X Pictures/Thinkstock

Comstock/Thinkstock

"We, who are so schooled in the art of listening to the voices of others, can often hear our own voice only when we are alone . . . For many women, the first choice, then, is to give ourselves the necessary time and space in which to renew our acquaintance with our lost voice, to learn to recognize it, and to rejoice as we hear it express our truth."
—FLORENCE FALK

• • •

"Your own words are the bricks and mortar of the dreams you want to realize. Your words are the greatest power you have. The words you choose and their use establish the life you experience."
—SONIA CHOQUETTE

• • •

"One's life has value so long as one attributes value to the life of others, by means of love, friendship, and compassion."
—SIMONE DE BEAUVOIR

• • •

"Our attitudes toward retirement, marriage, recreation, even our feelings about death and dying may make much more of an impression than we realize."
—EDA J. LESHAN

• • •

"Wherever you find a great man, you will find a great mother or a great wife standing behind him—or so they used to say. It would be interesting to know how many great women have had great fathers and husbands behind them."
—DOROTHY L. SAYERS

• • •

"I know enough to know that no woman should ever marry a man who hated his mother."
—MARTHA GELLHORN

• • •

"I'd much rather be a woman than a man. Women can cry, they can wear cute clothes, and they are the first to be rescued off of sinking ships."
—GILDA RADNER

• • •

Digital Vision/Thinkstock

"A friend of mine wrote recently, and said, 'It's a great life, if you don't weaken, as my grandmother used to say.' The images that conjured up were somewhat terrifying, but it reminded me of my own grandmother, who was definitely a low-comfort woman. If you complained about anything, she'd say, 'From the day of your birth, 'til you ride in a hearse, there's nothing so bad that it couldn't be worse.' My mother remembered a day in childhood when she ran inside, crying to my grandmother, 'Nobody loves me and my hands are cold,' and my grandmother said mordantly, 'God loves you and you can sit on your hands.' A hug and an 'I love you' might have been a wee bit more helpful. . . . Another friend's grandmother had more sensible advice. She used to say, 'Never trust a poseur.'"
—SARA PARETSKY

• • •

"Women may be the one group that grows more radical with age."
—GLORIA STEINEM

• • •

"Life is a bitter sweet journey my friend, a bitter sweet journey."
—LUELLEN HOFFMAN

• • •

"The most beautiful things in the world are not seen nor touched. They are felt with the heart."
—HELEN KELLER

• • •

"If you have knowledge, let others light their candles in it."
—MARGARET FULLER

• • •

"There is no greater insight into the future
than recognizing . . . when we save our children,
we save ourselves."
—MARGARET MEAD

• • •

"Life is what we make it, always has been, always will be."
—GRANDMA MOSES

• • •

Index